With love to Web for sharing a belief in
the power of bearing witness and to our girls,
Hannah and Iola, for laughing in the mud and the rain.— C.B.

To all the land mammals, birds, and other animals
living in the Arctic. — F.C.

Text copyright © Catherine Barr 2015
Illustrations copyright © Francesca Chessa 2015

First published in the USA in 2015 by Frances Lincoln Children's Books,
an imprint of Quarto Inc.,
276 Fifth Avenue, Suite 206, New York, NY 10001
www.franceslincoln.com

ISBN 978-1-84780-741-0

Illustrated with acrylics and colored pencil
Set in Myriad, Mrs Green, and Mountains of Christmas

Printed in Shenzhen, Guangdong, China

9 8 7 6 5 4 3 2 1

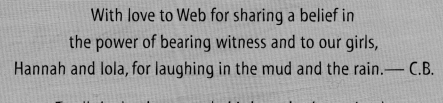

Elliot's
Arctic Surprise

Written by **Catherine Barr** ★ Illustrated by **Francesca Chessa**

Frances Lincoln
Children's Books

Elliot was on vacation by the sea.
He went for a paddle, and built a sand-whale.
It was fun, but what he *really* wanted was an adventure.
He lay on the sand and looked out at the sea.

Suddenly he spotted something in the water.
It was a bottle, spinning in the waves ...

Elliot caught the bottle and unscrewed the lid.
A curl of paper fluttered out onto the wet sand.

Elliot ran over to his mom and dad.
Maybe he was going to have an adventure after all.
  "Dad, can I go to the North Pole?" he asked.
  His dad smiled and nodded from behind
his newspaper.

Elliot ran toward the boats along the beach.
He wondered just how far away
the North Pole
could be.

A sunburned sea-captain took
the note that Elliot held out.
"Will you take me to find
Santa Claus?" Elliot asked.
"I want to HELP him."

The Captain smiled a big warm smile.
    "All aboard!" he said.
    Elliot helped untie the boat's heavy ropes
and they set sail for the North Pole.

Elliot hung on very tightly as the boat *raced*
across the sea. He grinned at the Captain.
This was going to be fun. He might not even
be back by bedtime.....

For a day and a night they flew across the waves.
When morning came, the Captain woke Elliot.
"Have a look outside," he said, with a wink.

It was incredible! They were surrounded by thousands
of other little boats, their bright sails flying past.
Elliot heard the **cheers** and **shouts** of children.
They all waved to him as they sailed by.

"Go on, boy, give 'em a wave! They're coming with us!"
laughed the Captain.

Elliot's eyes opened as wide as saucers.

He waved until his arms ached.

Together they all sailed on through the night.
It grew cold, and Elliot snuggled under
the Captain's coat to keep warm.
   "What will we do when we get there?" he asked.

But the Captain was quiet, staring into the dark seas ahead.
Elliot began to wonder if saving Christmas
might be difficult after all.

GIANT icebergs towered above them as they headed into the far north. The children were quiet now. Nobody was sure whether to be excited or scared.
    Elliot tucked his toes under another blanket, as they sped on through the icy waters.

Suddenly a tremendous **roar** rang out from the frozen land ahead. Icebergs *cracked* and *crashed* into the water. The children covered their ears and **shuddered**.

The boats stopped at the edge of the ice
and their colorful sails flapped
in the freezing winds.

The noises grew louder. Elliot gasped
as **GIANT black machines** loomed out of
the sea spray ahead.

There was a long silence.
A seabird *squawked*.
The water rippled as a seal dived
under the deep blue ice.

The Captain bent down.

"We're here," he whispered.

And suddenly Elliot knew exactly what to do.

As a giant engine spluttered,
he scrambled out onto the ice.
"**Stop!**" he yelled.

"STOP!"

Thousands of children surged after Elliot,
shouting at the machines. But their voices were lost
in the wind. The machines were so big and so frightening
that the children fell silent.

Millions of eyes blinked up at the **giant rigs**—
all set to drill for oil under the ice.

Elliot tried to sound brave.
"This is **Santa's home**," he said,
looking up at the man in charge.
"**Please** don't spoil it."

For a long time, the oil man stared out
at the children surrounding his machines.
He thought about his own little boy at home.
He thought about Christmas morning.

"*We'll go home,*" he said quietly.

"*We shouldn't really be here at all.*"

Everyone cheered, and the Captain stepped forward
to shake hands with the oil men. Then he threw his arms
in the air to wave at the children and **shout** with joy.
As he stretched up,
a button *popped* ...
then another ...
and his great coat swung open. . . .

The children stared in amazement.
The Captain was wearing a bright red suit
with white trim sparkling all around the edges.
Santa Claus!

Santa Claus thanked all the children
and began to sing . . .

*We wish you a merry Christmas,
We wish you a merry Christmas!*

The children and the oil men joined in
and their voices rose high and strong
above the wind.

They had saved Christmas—
for **ALL** the children in the world.

About the Arctic

Polar bears, reindeer, Arctic foxes, walruses, and narwhals live in the icy wilderness surrounding the North Pole. This stunningly beautiful place, the Arctic, is under threat from climate change and the rush for oil.

Climate change is melting the sea ice that wildlife need to hunt, rest, and breed; and drilling for oil in the Arctic risks massive oil spills that would be impossible to clear up. The use of oil as an energy source around the world is a major contributor to climate change.

Greenpeace is campaigning to halt climate change, protect the Arctic, and stop the rush for oil at the top of the world.

Find out more at www.greenpeace.org.uk/climate/arctic

John Sauven
Executive Director, Greenpeace UK